SOCIETY'S (LITTLE) TELEVISION
A COLLECTION OF SOLILOQUIES, THOUGHTS AND OTHER PROSE

KEITH LEVESQUE

Society's (Little) Television / @ Copyright 2022

Copyright

Society's (Little) Television: A Collection of Soliloquies, Thoughts, and Other Prose
First Edition Trade Book, 2022
Copyright © 2022 by Keith Levesque
All rights reserved. No part of this publication may be reproduced, stored in a retrieval system, or transmitted in any form by any means—electronic, mechanical, photocopy, recording, or otherwise—except for brief quotations in critical reviews or articles, without the prior permission of the publisher, except as provided by USA copyright law.
This book is a work of fiction. Names, characters, places, and incidents either are the product of the author's imagination or are used fictitiously. Any resemblance to actual events, locales, organizations, or persons living or dead is entirely coincidental and beyond the intent of either the author or the publisher.

To order additional books:
www.amazon.com (Digital E-book, Paperback, and Hardcover Available)

Published by Keith Levesque

ISBN: 979-8-9857986-0-9 (Digital/E-book/EPUB)
ISBN: 979-8-9857986-2-3 (Paperback)
ISBN: 979-8-9857986-1-6 (Hardcover)

Editorial: Kerry Wade, kerrywade.com
Book Design: Danny Montt, dannymontt.com
Formatting and Interior Book Design: Danny Montt, dannymontt.com
About the Author Photograph: Danny Montt, dannymontt.com
Proofreading and Endorsement: Spencer LoSchiavo, Stormworthy Records

https://open.spotify.com/
artist/0p2KhPJi3FLjBJr5pet1dV?si=pNqtWHWHRUW_qzMeMN-VwQ

Printed in the USA

Table of Contents:

Scene One:

Nebula 2
God Came Down in a Spaceship 3
The Trinomial Effect 4
The Origin 5
Xeno 6
Open Space 7
Little Planets 8
Expectations 9
Troubled Dynasties 10
Ancient Runis 12
All That Remains 13
Queen Mother 14
Winds, Waves, and Waters 15
Autumn 16
Electric Wire 17
Gaia Spring 18
Leisure Time in Spring 19
Spring time in Leisure 20
Promises and Treasures 21
Zen 22
Fields of the Elves, Cloves in Hand 23
Secrets in Reflection 24
The Bird and I 25

Scene Two:

The Caged Bird That Never Learned to Fly 27
A Nice Day at the Park 28
Particle Air 29
Sleeping Again 30
Sleeping Awake 31
The One or the Many 32
The Notion 33
The Inevitable Future 34
Mediocrity 35
Don't Think 36
Lighter Fluid 37
Metamorphosis Project 39
Narrow Minded Fear 40

Scene Two:

The Rally 41
The Machine 42
The Contemptible 43
A Slight Expertise in Journalism 44
Blessings of Fake Angels 45
A Child's Song 46
Cursed Generations 47
The Human Experience 48
Human Vending Machine 50
Locust People 51
Raise Your Spirits 52
Society's Little Television 53
The Leech 57
Paths 58
In the Passing 59
Dream 60
Squirrels 61
Keep the Pace 62
Believe in Something 63
Beautiful to Live 64
Precious 65

Interlude:

A Yearning 67
Saddened Eyes 68
One Starry Night 69
Observation 70
Two Ships 71
How Many Nights 72
Today 73
House of Windows 74
Take My Hand 75
Sweet Perpetuity 76
She Smiled 77
Jasmine and Plume 78
A Reflection 79
One Moment 80
When You Smile 81
Knowing, From Within 82

Scene Three:

A Harvest Never Grown 84
My Battered Ego 85
Lying in the Shadow 86
Phantoms 87
Selfish Suggestion..88
Lying on the Floor 89
A Young Man's Justice..90
The Box..91
Dry Rain 92
Clear Waters..93
Anything and Everything..94
Medallion 95
In Time, Eternal 96
Into the Morrow, I Sail...97
Waning Waters 99
Incomplete Me 100
A Memory 101
Photographic Memorial..102
Creeds of the Moniker, the Sobriquet, and the Omniest 103
Reverse Spin..104
The Fallen 105
Crystal Blue...106
Talking 107
The Pulse 108
The Urge to Break 109

About the Author..110
Additional Resources 111

Acknowledgments

A special thank you to Spencer LoSchiavo for proofreading and endorsing Society's (Little) Television, Danny Montt for book cover design, interior design, formatting and photography, and Kerry Wade for her great insight and editing,

I would also like to thank everyone who has supported me throughout the years and continues to do so. I dedicate this book to all of you.

Thank you.

Introduction

Trudge on. Sail on. Fly.
Have the urge to break free!

Welcome to Society's (Little) Television.

It's amazing to me what we as humans do to each other. I have seen the pain through my experiences and observations, and there has been a lot of it, both internal and external alike. From wars on religion to the terrible tragedies of racism, from greedy overlords to the current state of our planet, we have dealt with a lot, but we have always persevered.

As a child alone with my thoughts I often delved into dark thoughts, going over all the pain humanity has faced since the beginning of time; but such is survival, and we have survived. It wasn't until I traveled and encountered such a wide array of people from all walks of life, that I realized life isn't just all doom and gloom. These experiences helped me to look inside and crawl out of my darkness and into the light, following a path towards redemption, awareness, and self-improvement. It was a slow start, but better late than never.

This book, Society's (Little) Television, is an accumulation of those experiences and observations. We all have the capacity for good, to love and be loved, and to do our own introspection towards self-improvement—all for the better.

I hope as you read this book you will watch the past, as if on an old television, and embrace a more prosperous future for yourself and humanity; there is always hope, redemption, and enlightenment; no matter who you are or where you have come from. We are all in society's (little) television together.

So grab your cup of coffee, tea, or whatever beverage you prefer; put down that phone, turn off that television, and tune in to Society's (Little) Television . . .

Nebula

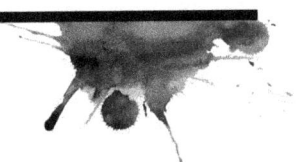

What compels us to live
Animal drive or instinct
Perhaps the mere mental satisfaction
The experience of simply living
Lie on my feet, stand on my head
Burst at the sides and scatter
Conform, turn into nebula matter
My eyes inverted now, this intricate vertebrate
Human flesh where inner prowess confined
Moving through the vastness
Some cosmic force drawn together
In the circuity of the mind
Open the mind, free the spirit
Strewn apart we all come together
No use in fighting it, it all consuming
Deep within the void, thoughts embroiled
Embracing fragility this mortal coil
In the dying, another it creates
The beginning forms from the other's end
Alpha and Omega, gravity pushes it together
Compelling us to live and to love
Life into death, turning us
All into nebula matter

God Came Down in a Spaceship

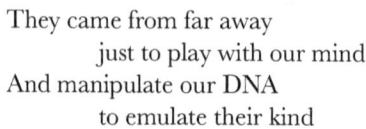

They came from far away
    just to play with our mind
And manipulate our DNA
    to emulate their kind

They kissed our lips, dipped our hips
    and welcomed us to our coming of age—
Not the time of adulthood
    that was already there—
The coming of age as wheat grows
    into the cereal we eat for breakfast

In the shades of Eden
By mystic rivers
The everlasting light fades
By mystic rivers
The silence sleeps

First, there was only water here
    then came the ground
Things held dear
    our legs grown into walking
Just trials and tribulations
experiments to grow
They made us from all the animals
    to infuse their skyward purpose
We are their evolved primates and mammals
    we eat, sleep, and kill like them
        have sex like them too

The Trinomial Effect

The eye of the trinomial effect
    caught in the thirteenth zodiac
    consumed by the face of the universe
    moving in triple time to the sound of breathing

The galaxy waxing and waning
    its smile of complexity
    perplexed by its own thoughts
    and the universe conceptualizes being

Ultimate truth gives birth to reality
    mapping knowledge and predetermination
    with each inhalation, birth brings death
    and death, reborn, giving hope to determination

In the falling the other stands
    in the fading the other grows
    and with great aspiration
    the choice is made . . .

. . . even in choosing nothing.

The Origin

The origin grows
All things are never
What they seem
To be what they seem

        There is depth
        Deep within where
        Eyes can't see
        In the broken pieces
        Of choices never made

Bring back the pieces
To the way
They ought to be
Deep within where
Eyes can't see

        Glower, unstable origin
        Collect and connect
        All the pieces
        And watch them grow . . .

Xeno

Memory, faded
Uncontrollable
Nothingness
A phenomenon
Into the desert space
Adrift and broken
A wasteland dried
The crimes of the forgotten
God a question
War answered
A thousand times

Timeless sand
Lived within a lie
A lie now found
Long since forgotten
Screams of the fallen
Emanate, no sound
Created by God
A God created
Fabrication
Alleviation
Left without a trace
Another dead rock
Floating in
Space

Open Space

Stare
Stare into the void
The open space
Lights going
Into
Out of
The eyes open
While stilled closed
Flashing
An eye within an eye
Within the colors
Looking back at me
Going in
Too soon
Control, lost
Encasing
Flowing
Now in a blackened space
The colors remaining
Steadily going
The taste to stardom
A sickening dizziness
Floating
Twirl and circle
Circle within circle
No longer a dream
Eyes open
Still closed
Gazing
The open space
Home
Comfort
Grand
Awake

Little Planets

How many people do you think are out there?
Living their lives, the only way they know
And how many of them have you met or seen
Out of all those places you've never been
In their own communities, their own worlds
A billion little planets nurturing life
At the right distance from the sun

Space and time, fate or destiny
These coincidental links seem to travel far

Expectations

In times of trial

Under skies holding stars

Like all things looking up

I have learned

They hold us down

Troubled Dynasties

The old, wise Tzu on the lonely mountain
        courted by the Singing Swan of tranquility
Half remembering the remains of a life lived
        she, soothing the troubled souls of her children—
Doused in circles to the glee of their rhythmic moods
        these spirits watch over and over and over
The events play out, they can't control
Rising waters, climatic storms
They feel the resonance, in the eye
        from crow and Old Crone, dancing in the forest
While the whaling Paranoid Oyster and Schizoid Pearl
        is heard throughout the realm, sharing their shell
        kingdom, with little emotion

Who is this so narcissistic and histrionic?
Oh! but Paranoid Oyster, the eldest son
Riding on his seventh wind, seventh attempted
Where is Schizoid Pearl?
Playing many roles, as she does, is not here to be found
She waits for this seventh act to play out
Perhaps she waits at mother Swan's grave
Whilst eldest son goes to play with father

All dressed up, eldest son, this high-born jester
        attempts yet again to claim his legitimacy
Adorned for father to play, an exquisite Earthly meal,
        to play at politics and take what would be his, too soon
Disregarding sister and mother's wishes

continued...

Father, old and decayed, his kingdom, frayed
        sits alone in his banquet hall
Son, Paranoid Oyster, high-born jester's meal is served
        this fine fished carp encased with underlying depression
Its accompaniments garnished and marinated
        with wild thoughts of grandeur
Here at the banquet hall, all is poisoned and perverse
        by the wisp of Old Crone's whiskers
The golden platter and silver spoon
        presented and disguised tribute and fealty
Father emperor and the mandate of heaven
eats, sister weeps, the jester waits

Mother, mother, father, father sweet daughter calls
Left to raise the children while the kingdom falls
Ambition and greed, son, like son before, repeats
        a story told a thousand times
Fades to the song of the Swan cradled in her melody
        where all things eventually, are left to reside, in tranquility

Ancient Ruins

An entire ocean mingles with ancient beginnings
Civilizations decaying in the passage
Of time soil rich with tender care
Plowed by a thousand ghosts working
To pull the very earth into the next harvest

An entire ocean mingles with ancient teachings
Civilizations decaying in the passage
Of time when the fisherman set sail
Farm rich in ghost fed food
Giving time to blacksmith and hardened steel

Forged weapons and steel hot skills
Navigate the waters
Irrigate the crops
A harvest of experience
Becoming the knowledge of books
Civilization grows
As the troops march on
Civilizations decays in the passage of war
An entire ocean mingles with ancient ruins

All That Remains

Down and down and down we all go
Bodies upon bodies
We are burning and burning

We wait
And we wait
Never lifting a finger
Until only
Our remains will linger

Plastic upon plastic
Too little too late, we think it's enough
To the seas and to the skies all the greed and the lies
Growing fatter and fatter while the whole world dies

We wait
And we wait
Never lifting a finger
Until only
Our remains will linger

We wait

And we wait

And we wait

And we wait

And we wait…

Queen Mother

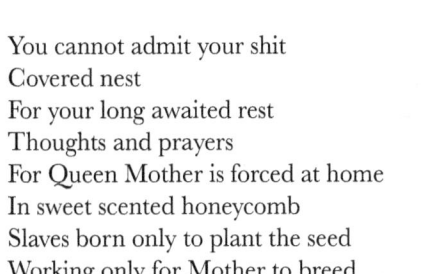

You cannot admit your shit
Covered nest
For your long awaited rest
Thoughts and prayers
For Queen Mother is forced at home
In sweet scented honeycomb
Slaves born only to plant the seed
Working only for Mother to breed
But in the face of the spirit
Or of the father, or of the son
Can what was once made
Become undone?
For the sons and daughters we grieve
Queen Mother can never leave

Winds, Waves, and Waters

The mist makes the day, sends her on her way
The sky sings a prayer while the white sea snaps
The old lady there, life near ending
Her feet in the soft land of the mainland by the harbor walls
Waiting for the tattered ships to come in
To tell her tales of where they've been
Something is brewing in those darkened clouds
The storm in the old lady's stare
Far off into the horizon washes slowly to the sea
Wind, wave, and water toy with old battered ships
The old lady there, her life nearly through
A life of experience buried beneath her wrinkles and the sand
May yet soothe and calm the winds, waves, and waters
The mist made the day and sent her on her way
The sky snapped a prayer while the sea sung farewell

Autumn

The grass still green, the sky less blue
Perplexed and contemplative
The world shies away towards the moon

Whirling winds tell, amongst themselves, lofty soliloquies
Puzzled and amused, trying to taste winter
Hot to cold, dangling over the swaying Earth
It spinning to hide away from the sun
In hopes of dancing in the long nights with the moon

As the watchful wallowing willows tickle
The air, so fair, makes the winds giggle in kindness
A lover caught between
All the while the trees cry, no more birds on their branches
In the wake of winter's frost the Earth and moon's affair
To them, it will always be, autumn

Electric Wire

Through the pavement sprout leaves of grass
Droplets of rain fall to quell the burning trash
Trees overcome electric wire
Growing over what we could not find
Under growth of the human kind
Balance the equilibrium and reprimand
Decaying frailty, not one remains
Over growth covers the city plains
Pulling, rips down electric wire

Cool blue florescence
Flickers on artificial markings
An altered topography
Lost to the vines

They tried to bind what binds them
They tried to kill what gives them life
They tried to strangle all with electric wire
But nature grew up between the pavement

Gaia Spring

The cool crisp spring breeze rolls in
Casting aside winter's chill
The trees burst with life, flowers illuminate
Keep the winter's cold still
With color, a frenzy of yellows, reds, and violet

Petals dance in the silken dew
Carried by the winds to lull the world to sleep
The winds comb their hands through Earth's green hair
Remembering all the promises they kept

Still the winds push whirling waters
And the rolling rivers
Greeting the rocks, these waters blue
Brimming with life, purifying
As the hills, valleys, and mountains glitter
And guide the wind and water

Guiding, back home, to Earth, to Gaia
It is spring, and only spring, that reminds the Earth
Old friends passing, gliding and changing

Gaia calls to her loved ones

Leisure Time in Spring

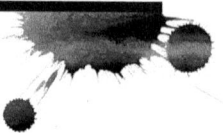

In spring newts and frogs
Slip into the darkness of the night

Guitars hum a melody that cracks the dawn
Soft wind blowing hair, singing in leisure

The frogs and newts crooning from their hiding places
Laughter ever over this leisure time in spring
To see what this night may bring

Spring Time in Leisure

Just after dark
Gazing at the stars
A brisk chill
Just by the sand
My lady nearby
Combing her hair
With my hand
A smile, so sure
To make me
Make happy this time
This moment
Here and now
The heavens broke
Telling of love
To come
To pass
And so too
        did spring

Promises and Treasures

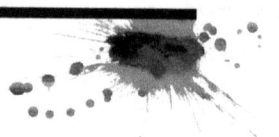

Spring's flowers in bloom
Summer's sweet careless rain
Autumn's abundant harvest
Winter's wind white snow
The promise of them
They make you, make you ever so beautiful
In all and every one of those things
They always come back to you

Zen

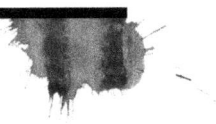

Watch the cherry blossoms, silken and shimmering
Sleeping within spring's soothing breeze
Entangled amongst themselves, themselves amongst
The hills and valley seeped in snow
I, watching, high and proud like the mountains
This drama turns the white snow red, cascade
Piercing the skies, leaving its mark
Upon each body and every blade

Scattering sun as the clouds break
Caught in the fore winds, heroic tales
Conquests and whispers of sweet nothings
Where is sublime seclusion? Asks the winds
Blades of men and blades of grass
Point to me, point home

Fields of the Elves, Cloves in Hand

Come walk with me and the unicorns
Among the cloves with five petals
Lay with me in the sway of fields and plains
Wish with me on the luck of fantasies
Wake with me with all your dreams come true
Watch with me, the little elves
Among the cloves with five petals
Follow me, to be, in a land of wonder
Among the cloves with five petals

Secrets in Reflection

Fingers running down white porcelain
Push away to pull closer
    flush out what might have been
And now, never knowing
    face down on the tile
It looks back at you
    reflection shining
The white light
    florescence glowing
Revealing but a hint
    of what might have been

The Bird and I

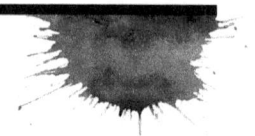

A bird sits on a branch
Nestled in the tree
I looked at her
And she stared back at me

Time passed by we had nothing to say
We could keep each other company if we both stayed

We both wore blue
She, the color of the sky
Me and my sorrow
The reflection in her eye

I looked at her as she looked at me
Or a new destination into the vastness, maybe

With a chirp she said hello
And with a nod I said goodbye

Scene Two

The Caged Bird That Never Learned to Fly

I only ever wanted a warm embrace
Only to get a kick in the face
I ask myself, why do I even stay awake
Need to close my eyes just to catch a break

All the stress from the things I do not know
Tried to put it all away and let it all go
But I was cut too deep, never breaking free
He gave me no love or empathy

Lashing out to kill the pain with crime or drug
Craving attention, a kiss or a hug
To hide from one hand too many, a broken past
Keep running, to make my childhood last

A moment longer, the moment before the cage

One more chase, another needle, soul mended
Mask after mask, a child's mind pretended
Never knowing love or ever breaking through
Following the sins that preceded me

Pain, pain, hit by hit, to kill what lies inside
Protect the child within before it dies
Endured cut after cut, a final goodbye and farewell
Lock myself away, to rest,
My final cell

A Nice Day at the Park

It was a nice summer day at the park
Though our morals and parents seldom stayed
The fires burn wild from just one spark
Through our lives the others played

They cannot see whom I want to be
They only see what they want of me

A fire barely raging, my soul
Kindled in the dying embers, fading memory a glow
Now left in the dying embers as they slowly burn
Near death, my sweet memories, ages ago
On the merry-go-round and around in turn

They only see what they want of me
Remembering… was there ever

A nice day at the park?

Particle Air

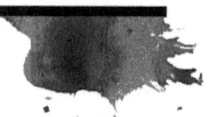

A bit here and pieces there
While the children play under the sun
Breathing in
Watching the followers
Watching those who criticize us
For all that we have done

The particle air
That bit by bit
Builds me so
Warms me up
Cools me down

Sipping from the cup
Thinking this is reality
Thinking are my friends,
My mother, and father
Looking over me

Criticizing all that I have done

Sleeping Again

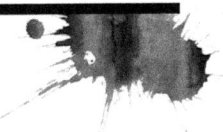

Simmer down the rumbling boil
Free the inner turmoil
Try and seek and find
Don't call me weak
As I continue to pick locks to closed doors
Mindful of what my subconscious has in store
In my own head the past
Comes to terms with my war-torn self and makes the clasp
I've been sleeping while I walk, again
I can't even think straight
Now my mind and pride shakes and shakes
Battered and bruised, I've been sleeping, again
Sleeping awake

Sleeping Awake

A dreamless dream, that inevitable itch
The seamless seam, that invisible stitch
Demoralize and excommunicate
The need to want to hate

Back stabbing and laughing
A caring mom still searching
For what was never had

Lusting for more and more
Picking locks to closed doors
Staying calm, taking a breath
Statues of guilt and fear and clay

Soaking it all up like a sponge
Ringing out the pain only to gather it all up again
Living asleep, sleeping awake

Red-eyed and lonely, only dreams
Goals, truths, and lies
Like all moments and potential lives
Go by unanswered
Unaccounted

The One or The Many

I dreamed of one, to choose the many
Little grains of sand slipping
Little grains that flip and spill off my finger tip

As the ebb and flow of the tide washes them all away
Here I stand, empty handed, myself reprimanded
With nothing good or fair, just a memory once there

The Notion

Pending, on the notion
Silk tongue of deceit
Where two faces meet
One for each situation
Approach and diffuse
Behind every pretension
The notion to use
The target your eye
Once had, crave no more
Hide the perfect lie
Just to get what you came for

The Inevitable Future

Can you see where you're going
With your eyes full of greed and hate?
Can you know where you're going
With your mind lost?

You love what I hate
Hate what I love
Only to kill both you and I
Drowning now, fools in blood

It doesn't matter, unless you care
These trained children
Love what we hate
Hate what we love
Is it too much to handle
To just leave the other man alone

Earth, are only chance at life
Let us not lose it
(To no one's fault but your own)
Let's come together
Love what we love
Think of your children
Our only future

Mediocrity

Aslant now and sweetly medicated
Take any pill I choose

One for color
One for mood
One on a whim
Just to make me feel
One for health
One for a thrill
One may promote death
Another keeps my mind still

By the things I buy
So dedicated

One for my head
One to make me loud
One brings me down
Another makes me proud
One for size
One for a thrill
One for the body
Another keeps my mind still

Sticking together broken packs
Just hoping to get by and survive
On someone else's future

Don't Think

Ignorance is indeed bliss
Let those I trust
Hold my leash
Let those I love
Carry my emotions
Let my friends
Come for fun
And let my parents
Tell me what to dream
I would be
Happier
Free

Lighter Fluid

The controlled queue for their place in time
Take the placebo pill in waiting
The man sits in the window, panel, screen
Watching his puppets play
Changing what might have been

Gather around and join
The man says to the fire
Cigarette resting on his pouting lips
Time to light you up and smoke you out

Disrupt your point of view
Make you think what you think you do
What you thought you knew
Choosing what you chose
Disguised as choice, already chosen

The controlled watching a screen
The big man in the mask
Telling his puppets what they want
Through ever changing voices and faces
Changing logic, changing reason

Gather around and join
The man, the fire, the sweating glands
Love the sound of his own voice
Victims of the dead never had a choice
Mouths cost too much to feed
Unless they serve a purpose

A sudden gesture or the trick of the eye
Controls the growing mass
He calculates future events
Have already happened in the past
Filling in the void and gaps of mind

continued...

Repeating, never reading between the lines
The controlled a full subscription
Of overrated superstition

Do what they do to you, to do to them and back again
Think what they thought for you
Your precious life and greedy gain
Is the man really the only one to blame?

Gather around and join
Be a part of the fire
The pyre of liars
A slow roasting brew of you
Drip, drip, right into his pocket

What could be reality may be false
What is false could be true
Believe what the big man tells you
Ignorance is bliss and the honey sweet

Metamorphosis Project

Call my name
When the fighting starts

Program me
To be your tool

Put your chip inside
By your words alone
Metamorphosis time
Seizing my mind
Rebuilding my face

Call my name
Birthed to a new identity

It fits me well
Their working fool

Artificially created for the likes of Man
But God will not comply
Metamorphosis, war has come
I, the mindless drone
By the chromosomes torn

Call my name
But I will not be there
When the fighting starts
I will remain
Human ID intact

Narrow Minded Fear

It seems to me that no one knows
Why people come as fast as they go

They criticize what lies in me
Never criticizing the things they do

I see their faces in all my fears
They criticize the other to hold back tears

They fear what they not know, so they claim
But they fear what lies inside
They fear what is the same

The Rally

Standing with a sign
In all kinds of weather
Yelling for maybe rights of mine
Solidarity, leaderless herd
Protesting for anything that matters
Misrepresented and misspelled on a wooden post

Change as we want it, may never come
Or perhaps it all changes but in the wrong way
It may only benefit the lucky few, unlucky

The Machine

Working for the machine
That dictates our every move
No mediator for the mind
And the hands
The high-born in power
The only ones who taste the fruit
The fruit, reaped by machine controlled workers
Toiling for the higher
Bridge the gap from mind to hands
Differentiate from machine and man
There needs to be a mediator
For society to prosper
Together
As one, in unity

The Contemptible

Solemn promises seldom made
By those without virtue
Through obligations they seek to prosper
Hands clasped, cold smiles
They trick themselves to feel good
A small gesture to drop the cliché
With a how do you do or I am here for you
Such knaves, to get only what they desire
But without, such contempt, I suppose
There would be no need to create heroes

A Slight Expertise in Journalism

Unravel to quell the voices in my head
Weary of the wind, battering window
Slightly swaying, revealing what I've done
Am I paranoid about the things I've said

Prose running down a wall of tile
While a cap falls to the floor
Not even an ounce of inclination
Of being true or politically correct
I call my dad a drunk, write whatever's on my mind

When I told them to fuck themselves
I thought I could do better
If I were president, thank god I'm not

My point of view is skewed, scrawled in the stall
Providing provocative suggestions
Stories and one liners, illustrate the walls
Right next to all the people I can call

Racist, sexist, homophobic
Sadistically and maliciously out of their tree
Some have a slight expertise in journalism
Others gossip – rumors, hearsay, and other views
Rather than be in the places they should be

If we are in a free country, why is nothing free
So many question their rights
Question each other's conspiracies
Question freedom of speech, sick of society controlling
Through the eye-hole on the door
Who is this that's sly and sleek to take a peek
And who am I in isolation in a public place
Who puts the pen to the wall, to scrawl
Out of the bathroom stall?

Blessings of Fake Angels

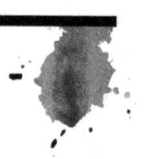

A puddle of blood
Trickling down a street
Mother and father cry
As the blood greets their feet

To mask their demons
They curse their sons
Lock-up their daughters
Hiding deeds unforgotten

In both fear and hope
They send their kindred
In hopes of breaking free
Only to bury their dread

As time passes on
The emotional debt due
They'll groom another
And push them too

A Child's Song

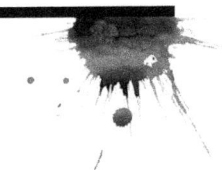

I want to live where the water flows
Lying in the grass that never grows

I want to be in the sky
Soaring with all the birds that never fly

I want to be able to feel this love
That fills the underground

I want to show you a love that you can see
Mother, thank you for all the tears you cried

I will shine on and on and through
Because of you

I, child, lying in the grass
And never grew

Cursed Generations

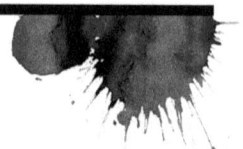

Was life that awful
Choosing not to live
Caught in the middle of it all
Someone else's baggage
I now must carry
For simply sharing DNA
Even after age, they never fade
These dogs and demons
Biting and clawing at my feet
Before I could ever run
Dying before ever born

The Human Experience

Throughout history people have been saying
The same old thing, and people still refuse to listen
From their comfort zone, their beloved bubble
Being human, a human being as it were
is an interesting thing . . .

We want material things for power, wealth, and social status
or something just to keep us all occupied
We want to explore but must have someone
hold our hand the whole way through
We want to find love where perhaps
love cannot be found

I have seen this, experienced this
taking it all in from day to day
all the way to the big picture and back again
Really using the power of insight, the power of observation
looking without and within
life, humanity, the self...

Accomplishing next to nothing in the grand scheme
Waiting day in and day out to love or be loved
Watching it all fade
A fallen friend, a troubled family member
A love long past, a youth long gone
Truths half forgotten

continued...

But such is life, to fight, to live,
To stand on our own
Better things always come
The calm breeze after a storm
Stop, think, feel, share our suffering
We could all heal together

Our next step, our next goal, our new mindset
To be one again, to be ourselves
Never complete, never perfect
If just for a moment, the path is clear
The frequently found, and held onto
We all heal together

Human Vending Machine

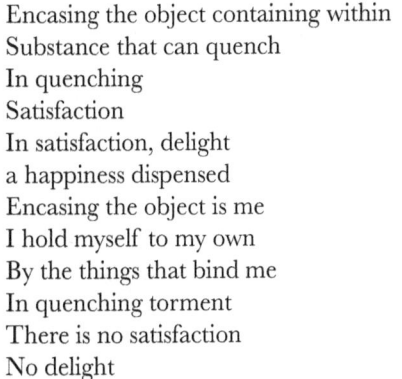

Encasing the object containing within
Substance that can quench
In quenching
Satisfaction
In satisfaction, delight
a happiness dispensed
Encasing the object is me
I hold myself to my own
By the things that bind me
In quenching torment
There is no satisfaction
No delight

Locust People

The people squirm
The people crawl
Cleaning mind cobwebs
Slithering worms
As dead bugs fall
Past and present entwined

In the darkness demons brought
The light of reason, worms distraught for guilt remaining

Screaming out
The moth entangled in the flame
Knowing that it's children
Will be the same, in flame
Only the worms and

The locusts cry
Leaving famine while the others die

Raise Your Spirits

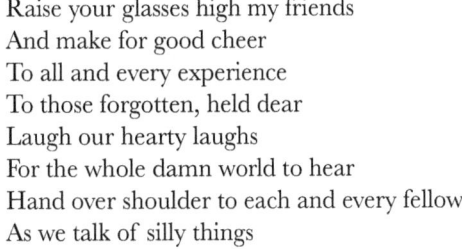

Raise your glasses high my friends
And make for good cheer
To all and every experience
To those forgotten, held dear
Laugh our hearty laughs
For the whole damn world to hear
Hand over shoulder to each and every fellow
As we talk of silly things

Raise your spirits
To all the good times
There are many more to be had
So think not of regret
We can drink to remember
We can drink to forget
Raise your glasses high my friends
As we talk of silly things

On and on and on we go
to drink away the sad
There's one there leaning against the door
We got another lying face down on the floor
So we drink and so we drink, there's no time to think
As we talk of silly things

Society's Little Television

We saw the skies swell up
    and the ground split, withered
Noises filled the restless sky
    bolts tore the earth
Fiery flakes of snow
    upon us who gazed at the blackened sun
The snow burned flesh
    upon us who starred in confusion
Insides seeped through gaping holes
    to rest and settle as deadened compost
    that which can no longer grow, may never grow again
And the others, those who were spared
    trembled insensibly
    there were no drugs to calm them
Twelve angles kissing the night
    as the awe-stricken disbelievers
    knelt and cried for the day

And as the time passed slowly
    on the decaying planet burned alive
Bloody compost could not fertilize what was lost
The scorched earth, faded civilizations, ancient ruins
    overused power
    made their own history
    repeating
They gave us a say, told us what not to do
Laws, institutionalized regulations
    created for control for all but the powerful
    who made, bent, and blended them
controlling and binding
We toiled on their soil, paid our dues and taxes
    so they could protect what is theirs
    our friends and families worn

continued...

Hate and greed that spawned war
    with smoke and fire, the lands were torn
Even the societies and religions
    could not keep the peace throughout time
Humanity built its castles and highest wall
    to protect the fact, that, in the end, we are only animals, after all
Sacred in our hearts, where we were once touched
    by the loss of our own, were once blessed

And so heroes were born of mist, of legends, of myths
From the coziness and comfort of our homes
    we were told of such stories, sang lullabies
And when we did calm in the dead of night
    we closed our eyes and dreamed fantastic
Dreams of unrivaled heroes
    wild-eyed satyrs playing in the moonlight
lakes filled in precious gems
    a fair maiden, who cries pearls
    clad in silk and elaborate thread
    tip tapping in triple time

Perseverance and determination
Just to live for one more day
such is the resolve of mortal men
Well hope is hope
I suppose that's all that's left

The angels of creation and destruction
    bestowed unto the greatest of heroes
Luminous
the sword of purity and of light
    encased in the light, return to the night once plagued
Always at the ready, always at the vanguard
    he wins all battles with wit hardened steel

continued...

Hindsight and foresight, triumphant
    honor, respect, and sincerity
And this great hero, heart ignited
    walks among friends and fellow heroes and
She, his counterpart, the sheath to his sword
    muse for his passion, reasoning, and resolve

His equal, and no other
One heart, one love
Credibility and kindness
They walk side by side, in parallel
Their strengths and flaws equal
Of a man, of a woman, to be human
Sacred in their hearts

In passing through the channels
Faded idealists desperately try
To become
They wish to emulate
That separates us from reality and fantasy

Reality harshly tore my insides out
For such heroes are scarcely found if even found at all
For there would always be troubled times
Faded heroes, archaic stories, told
Merely for a sense of contentment, of hope
To be kept away until sleep, in our dreams
To trick a life of mediocrity and contentment
To wildly hope, chasing the frivolous
With television
Cold calculated computer, human intelligence
For money and materialistic wealth while the wells run dry
Electricity, oil, war… such magnetism
Force us to collide and conform

                                              continued…

To clone, to create, man into machine
An artificial existence
Content with false security
That personifies our insecure delusions
These man made illusions…
And so the twelve angels call
      nuclear, human waste, the fiery flakes fall

I was hardly there, if even there at all
Hiding in the hollow heart

I tried to mend the unmendable society
I tried to calm the skies
So we could see the sun
I tried to heal our Earth
So we didn't have to run
I tried to cool the ice and the water
So we didn't have to drown
I tried to mend our broken minds and hearts
So they wouldn't bring us down
And I had hoped

I had hoped to find happiness and peace
For you and I, for humanity, in our time
Waiting for a long-winded melody
I am no hero, no sword or light
Only the blackened sun of the ever night
I need no lullaby
Before my deepest sleep

The Leech

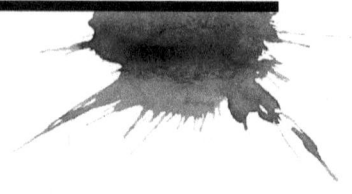

And who are we?
To hang to a moment
To hang to a memory
To have this life lived content
In complacency
In mere mediocrity
We leech
To hold on to every waking word
To keep what we have become now
Sucking dry our insides

We've reaped what we've sown heavy
Each and every one of us carries a stone
In the weight of it all, we will all drown

Who are we?
To believe in everything
Never questioning anything, nothing
A life chasing something
Only to wallow away
In insecure delusions

Only after we fall, we'll realize
Our happiness, small
We were never comfortable
Every passing breath
One more second closer to death
Another life lived in content
Another dull day spent
Sucked dry and still hungry
Hanging on to the memory
Realizing how we were, never really comfortable
Never really happy at all

Paths

One will choose the path of defiance
in one place they will never stay
One will choose the path of compliance
taking orders day by day
One will choose the path of justice
clinging to ideals in their heart
One will choose the path of salvation
solemn promises make amend
One will choose the path of self-medication
tearing dreams and families apart
Some will choose the path they chose
while others cling to paths they never want

In the Passing

Sway
As the wind blows

Bend
We pass the time

Without care
Happy, awhile

With our feet on the ground
We hear

The Earth's reaffirming voice
To what we've found

Life, steady on, steadily goes
As the wind blows

We pass the time…
Earth and space, everlasting

A trifle, living
Becomes a treasure in the passing

Dream

We must learn to animate our emotions

So that we may see

Before the dream is gone

Squirrels

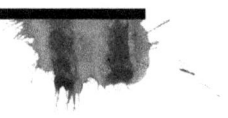

The grass sways
Against the wind
Squirrels collect the remains
Of autumn's harvest
Leaves slowly fall
Crisped and curled

The humans make way for each other
The women, for those they say they never want
The men, for those who come the easiest
The squirrels for winter nuts
As the grass takes in the silken dew of morning

Keep the Pace

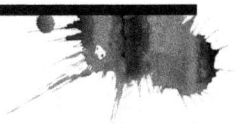

Keep the pace
Keep going
Learn from mistakes
Feel the wonder of a child
Save moments
Try to slow time
Memories are the keys
To unlocking the future
The things then
Reflect now
Try to slow time
Savor memories
Feel the wonder of a child
Learn from mistakes
Keep going
Keep the pace

Believe in Something

Trace back the steps and see where they go
Spiraling into the past
Reawakening what I may know
Have I arrived, at last?

The past can hold so much pain
Tumbling over my own feet again
Does it always end this way
Are they any sweet memories left
To drive me on
To live and to love
To believe in
I must believe in something

Spiraling down into the void, memories lied
Caressing a faint light of hope, to mend
It reawakens all the times I should have cried

Following the steps
Spiraling into the past
Embracing what might have been
What could be
Eyes see clearly
To believe
In something believe
In something

Beautiful to Live

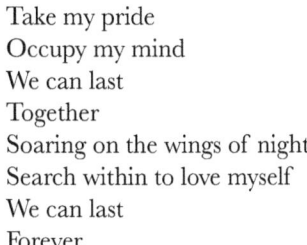

Take my pride
Occupy my mind
We can last
Together
Soaring on the wings of night
Search within to love myself
We can last
Forever

Motivating me to do great things

To die for a cause
To live for a future
To cure it all
To bend the time
To stop the past
From happening again

Motivating me to do great things

With a smile
And with my love
I give myself something good
To die for
To make it beautiful
To live

Precious

If we are precious, and I know we are
To the ones who love us and to ourselves
Why feel unnecessary pain
Our internal struggles
Illusions brought by external delusions
Cast aside comparisons and judgment
Love and be loved!

Our morals, ideals, and deeds, motivating
Upheld with the utmost respect and discipline
Upheld with the utmost sincerity and clarity
Throughout our daily intentions and interactions
We can show our worth and resolve
We will know what it means to be precious
Love and be loved!

A Yearning

Bombarded day in and out
Digital trash
Ticking of the clock
Time ticking past
A flood of lethargy washes over me
Then leaves
In my stupor I see the static haze
Flashing in and out
A warning sign from a broken lighthouse
Beckoning ships long since sailed
More of the same
Touch the mirror, turn the dial
Remember to fake my smile
The routines and the motions
Until death
I'm pushed into the static, to swim with the trash
I never littered, not once contributed
Yet I must go on as such, all the same
More of the same
Sometimes, I get a glimpse of a clearing sky
But then I must wake, work, and sleep again
Slowly passing what little time
I yearn, yearn for something new
Love, perhaps

Saddened Eyes

I turn around and walk away
From the things that matter most
The things that make me tick

Look into those precious eyes
They made me happy
They made me cry
They made me realize just who you are

I closed the door
And threw the key
To all the moments that made me
All the memories that make me

Look into those saddened eyes
I've broken a heart and someone cried
I was never there and I never tried
I was never in the queue
I never looked into those saddened eyes

One Starry Night

Where's a candle
Lying in the halt of time
I put the toys away
On one starry night
She smiled through her fingers
Simple in her sadness
As I ran through her fingers
I put all the toys away
I grew a little closer
A candle on a starry night
She leaned heavily on me

Observation

Watching
Staring
Observing
Through my eyes I
See what will come of me
Watching
Staring
Observing
For what happens
To you
Reflects what will happen
To me

Two Ships

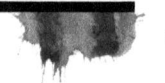

Some people go like two ships passing
In the night, but where to?
And some people will stay
And I want to know which are you
I need to know

A warm glow from the firelight
Warm like you
And like the stars in the sky
The glow can fade in the day
And I want to know which are you
I need to know

Some people go like two ships passing

How Many Nights

I can only imagine why
You don't feel the way I do
We're drifting away
Pretending by the standards of society
We could have had a chance
We fade away together
Yet alone

We watch our memories as they go
It's too late, the day's gone
Passing into the next, without a try
How many nights are we
Alone

You see only what I see
We're drifting away, away from ourselves
Pretending by the standards of society
Our words are failing
Pointing the finger at each other
Alone

Today

Today, I'm feeling down, today
I feel like I'm running out of myself
Today, I may have let myself down, today
It is and was always because of you
Today, I loved you then and I still do
Love you still and always will, today

Trudging and trudging through towards you
I don't know why or what else to do

Today, I want to be happy, today
Today, but I can't without you
Today, it's because of you, today
Today, I loved you then and I still do
If there was only a way, today

House of Windows

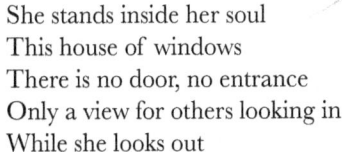

She stands inside her soul
This house of windows
There is no door, no entrance
Only a view for others looking in
While she looks out

With a sad smile
The windows are covering
Condensation, the heat within
The coldness from outside, smothering
Trying to reach out but can't reach in
Her soul dripping down her windows

No one can see
Through her foggy windows
She can't leave
And no one can enter
She can't see without
And no one can see within

Through this house of windows
Through her soul
Without a door

Take My Hand

If I could see clearly
I would search for inner truth
If I could listen more soundly
I would hear your beck and call
If I could love more purely
I would love only you
If I could have a steady hand
I would lend it to achieve our dreams
If I had more kindly lips
I would softly touch them to yours
If I could call myself a lover

If you could see clearly
Would you see me in your heart?
If you could hear more soundly
Would you hear my loving words?
If you could love more purely
Would you love truthfully?
If you could have a steady hand
Would you keep my ring upon it?
If you had kind lips
Would you choose kind words for me?
If you can truly say I do, my lover
Then we could live this life together

Our lives lived in parallel
Our reflections, as one

Sweet Perpetuity

Can you see?
See...
What...

Can you hear?
Hear...
What...

Can you taste?
Taste...
What...

Can you feel?
Feel...
What...

The things...
What things?
The things that move you
In an endless...
...perpetuity

The things...
That drive you to live

The things...
In a person...
...you love
...so much...

She Smiled

The wind blew lightly
Lifting your hair
Your eyes glistening gems
Caught unaware

The winds and the rain
The sky and the sea
Hearing your name
Settle ever so calmly

The light of the stars
Several millions of miles away
Shine more brightly
With such radiance
All because of your smile
It warms my every thought
Some sweet gravity
Pulling, I am caught
In this sweet serenity
Smiling at you
Smiling at me

Jasmine and Plum

I close my eyes
Feel the rhythm of your body
To the beating of our hearts
Lying in the scent
Jasmine and plum
Skin like cherry blossoms falling
Tangle and weave, floating on the river, this bed
Our bodies here, entwined

A Reflection

A single glance
A single touch
It guides me
It graces me
Your hand of fate
Your presence
Your beauty
Angel light
Another touch
Another glance
Flowing hair like the silken mist of night

This gracefulness
In your eyes, reflect
Unto me, our sweet moment, transpire

Our reflection
Mirroring eyes
Our passionate love, our burning desire

One Moment

One moment, this one sweet moment
An eternity in time, spent
The night knowing what it is keeping
As dawn watches those now sleeping
Sun and moon, betwixt

A sweet scent from the previous night
Dances on my pillow on the dawning light
Silken skin on satin sheets, warm pressed
Hearts flutter to the rhythm once dressed
Two souls tangled, kissed

Warm breath thaws my heart
While, now, closed eyes dream apart
Cradled in the morn, I trust together
For even but a moment, we lay here forever
And but once, never missed

When You Smile

Sometimes I wake up at night
When I'm feeling cold
But when I think of you
It warms my soul

The sun smiles in your smile
And the moon shies away for awhile

It's all because of you
Of what's in your mind
And what's in your heart
It's all because of you

When you smile

Knowing, From Within

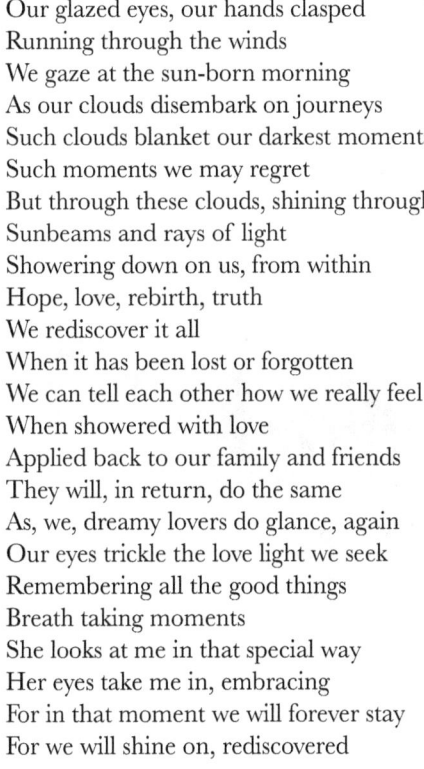

Our glazed eyes, our hands clasped
Running through the winds
We gaze at the sun-born morning
As our clouds disembark on journeys
Such clouds blanket our darkest moments
Such moments we may regret
But through these clouds, shining through
Sunbeams and rays of light
Showering down on us, from within
Hope, love, rebirth, truth
We rediscover it all
When it has been lost or forgotten
We can tell each other how we really feel
When showered with love
Applied back to our family and friends
They will, in return, do the same
As, we, dreamy lovers do glance, again
Our eyes trickle the love light we seek
Remembering all the good things
Breath taking moments
She looks at me in that special way
Her eyes take me in, embracing
For in that moment we will forever stay
For we will shine on, rediscovered

Scene Three

A Harvest Never Grown

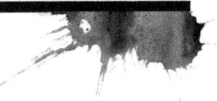

I toiled my days plowing seeds that never grew
Picking paths towards fortunes I thought I knew
But all my crops were gone when the harvest came
The passion withered, the dream had gone dry
I was left standing on barren ground

I wished to pick the right seeds and sharpen the tools
I wished for passion and abundance
To finally see the harvest of my own two hands

But I never sharpened the tools or picked the seeds
I never studied the land or listened to its dreams
I never changed the water or tended the soil
I worked and toiled and never listened
I was left standing on barren ground

Can I still make it right?
Before my breath goes dark
While I still see the light

My Battered Ego

I'm running on empty, too fast to slow down
There's no roadside station to fill me up
I just have a battered ego and an aching head
Too many things I've done, too many things I've said

My regrets are running up the speedometer
And my brakes are failing
Nowhere else for this road to go

This one-way crash course, of course
My battered ego has taken the wheel
I can't fill or warm it up, commonsense escapes
I'm going too fast to slow down
And I'm running on empty

Lying in the Shadow

I need to hide from myself
Need to hide from everyone else
Need to hide what needs to be hidden
Behind the charade I am never truly known

Untruthfully unrewarding
I realize I've become
Another casualty of circumstance
Hiding in the dark
Lying in the shadow

I can't feel
What makes me what I am
I didn't make their list
I am different from they
I am different from them
They only criticized what was the same inside

Hiding in the hollow heart
Hiding in the shallow mind

Lying in the shadow

Phantoms

Change tastes good when I'm eating toast
Contemplating my reality with every sip of juice
Reading the paper, my life the headline news

Can I chase away the phantoms that haunt
Show my brave new face to the world today
Head held high this glorious day

Can I feel the emotion and pain?
My heart, these muddled demons
Yesterday I walked away
My life the headline news
Comes back to haunt me
Again

Selfish Suggestion

Why don't you look my way
Is my smile too bold
I only come in search of what I need
I have no care for what you want
Words never come out right
When the goal is so close
This selfish suggestion
Of leaving nothing more than a trace
Of what could have been
Of what might have been

Lying on the Floor

Lying on the floor
Staring up
Reverse side of the revolving fan
Closed eyes slowly open
A reflection of memories
Half forgotten, half fade

These memories, half truths
Passing through a scene, a movie mind
Some created to make me happy
Some so trivial now
Some I never thought
Such problems then
Such regrets and anxieties

Lying on the floor
Staring at the fan
Trying to form the plan
Uncertainties creep in my head

Thinking of all the times I tried
All the times I failed
All the times I lied
To not bruise my sanity
All bad memories compressed
Holding back the ones
To be suppressed

Catch a beautiful scene in the spinning fan
Focus on the memories ahead
Wake up someone new

A Young Man's Justice

One man can hate everything, all that has been done by the other
Does he seek vengeance, dig two graves
One for himself and the other for who he seeks

One man can right the wrongs if inside himself he seeks the other
Wear the other's shoes, know their mind, know their actions

One man can shed the darkness, cultivate the change
To show himself his resolve, to encase himself
In the everlasting light cast on his two dug graves

The Box

Pushing through
Trying to break free
Aspiring for second best
What are we truly?
Living and dying
A mortal coil in a wooden box
Deep in the earth soil
Ever trying, always settling
Deep within the mind
The soul and the body
What am I really looking for?
What will I find?

Dry Rain

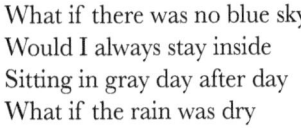

What if there was no blue sky
Would I always stay inside
Sitting in gray day after day
What if the rain was dry

Wandering, from year to year
Wondering, where I go from here

How the time would pass by, soaked
Feet in the puddle of dreams, unattainable

Clear Waters

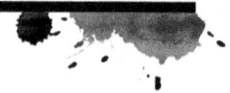

I see what I want to see
The far off world, the person I'd rather be
Sailing on through the human experience
I dream, I hope, I love this way

Where the grass snaps to the whistling winds
Where the cerulean sky entangles the mountains
Where the clouds gasp and cry
Where sweet serenity lies
Graceful as the falling petal

Where the cool breeze yearns to soothe
Where I embark across rocky waves and horizons gray
Where I gaze at the moon until the sun kisses the day
Holding intangible things in my hands
Encompassing the universe in every grain of sand

It is these things that move me
Move me to achieve great things in this human experience
And by doing this, still the waves
As I embark my sail on my journey

Anything and Everything

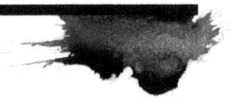

Anything and everything I do or say
Gets lost somewhere along the way
Every day and every year I lose my mind
I learn to use my time
Teetering on extremes
Anything and everything will be okay
I know I'll find my way
I know I'll find my way

Medallion

I roamed house to house, some took me in
But I scattered on the sight of fellows
All I had was a medallion of tarnished tin
I shimmered in the light, cascaded in the shadows
Both demons and angels residing within
As I pushed forward I saw a thousand paths passed
I felt the blood
The blood of those who suffer
Those who suffer from my hand or the other
I see the pain
Feel the pain
Everyone's experience, everyone's sin
This medallion of tarnished tin
So I walk on
If I can see through the shadows, see through the darkness
Then I can see that I am no longer the person of my youth
I am worthy of forgiveness; we are all worthy of forgiveness
All of the sin and all of the bad things to each and every human
By the blood of the fallen, I pave the road to righteousness
At last my medallion of tarnished tin, will glow, a diamond

In Time, Eternal

Eyes wide open
I can feel it
This new experience
Trembling senses
My mood moves me
Flowing through
Soothing and cool
Provision and retool
Accouter my mind, remember
This moment
This new experience
Keep this memory
Freeze it, dream it, live it
In time, eternal

Into the Morrow, I Sail

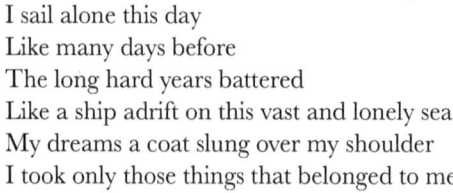

I sail alone this day
Like many days before
The long hard years battered
Like a ship adrift on this vast and lonely sea
My dreams a coat slung over my shoulder
I took only those things that belonged to me

I wanted to take those things
Inside me, even some of those never mine
Desires, and dreams
They were never mine to take
These are the things I sail for and I'm still searching
But how can I see through the fog
Told what I'll never have, never be

No note to play, no voice, no sound, this lonely melody
The birds could unbind and set me free
So that I can let it go

Where will I go until tomorrow?
Sail into the morrow behind the other eye
Waits yet, another lie
I can no longer feel what it is real
On this vast and lonely sea
To try and catch my fading dreams

continued...

Mother
Father
I am not coming home
I don't have one
I sail alone on
Winds of change will carry me
To treasures long forgotten
Carry me to the things I sail for
This time, not misbegotten
All my own
I'm still sailing
And I'm still searching . . .
Into the morrow

The sea cascades
Cradling the reflection of the moon
The sea splits, trailing tide
Yearning overhead, darkened cloud
It rains to wash away, the world spins

Wandering alone, to ask the question
Maybe find the self in the riddle secluded in time
I am born
The universe never asking why . . .

Waning Waters

Waters run
Trickle down
Collecting into puddles
Drops of rain
Will remain
Conform and collide
The reflections
Showing
My life
Purified
Soothing
Cleansing
Washing me away
My tides
Waning
I am changing
My memories
Abstaining
And rearranging
Resolutions
Sustaining
And maintaining
Waters run
And the ripple grows

Incomplete Me

I am not a being in my own regard
But a being of forced habits
In this I am forgotten, untold
My legacy, faded within

Everything, as I know it
From the microorganisms
To the elements of the universe
Come and go
Like the passing wind
Time crumbles and falls
Like the hearts that made it

I cannot exist here, among you
There is no choice
But to respectfully conduct rituals
Not my own

To conduct myself
In the "proper" way

A Memory

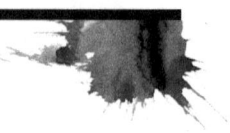

I am that was
Already come to pass
Ignored and forgotten
My insides perish slowly
Coming through the moment
Experience transpired
Wallowing in the illusions
Time brought
I am just a memory
Failing to fall with humility
Now I'm gone from here
No longer whole
A remnant
Of what was…
I am what was to be
Will you remember me?

Photographic Memorial

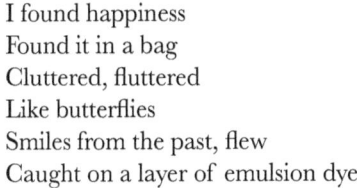

I found happiness
Found it in a bag
Cluttered, fluttered
Like butterflies
Smiles from the past, flew
Caught on a layer of emulsion dye

Some soothing, some disturbing
These tintype photo of the past
Touched
Remembering
Childhood friends
And the dreams we had

I let these butterflies free
Pour a drink to the fallen
To pay homage to the memory

And I am getting older
Soon, I too, will be another smile
Caught on a layer
Another butterfly to let free

Creeds of the Moniker, the Sobriquet, and the Omniest

How would I find salvation in an other's heaven?
Dictating norms atop their thrown
Held up by greed and power alone
Rules and regulations descended from on high
They fall like snow, no sense, no logic
Sin-wrapped teachings, pedagogic

Tilling the dirt, the other's mud on my face
A mockery to all that has been done
Civilization, as I know it, on the run
But they do not know how to run the races
They take my spirit, take my pride

I sleep, I plead, I weep, I cry
Following their "salvation"
And in my mind made to think a whole new way
Their creeds beaten into me
Shunning my every step, lack of independence
Wanting to live, even as a shell, listening to what they say!

Follower and lead, lead to believe
There is nothing here
The other's mud still on my face
There is no heaven
Only the particles in space
So why do I sit idly by thinking
there is life after death?

Reverse Spin

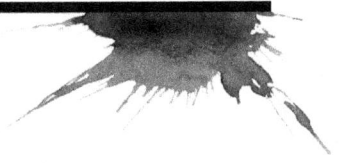

Every time I wake

The world is spinning 'round me

Never giving me the chance to get off

So, I'll run the other way

Just to catch myself

Slow the whole damn thing down

The Fallen

Close, and so far away
I wish I could be by your side
Shed my skin of clay
Shed my inner pride

I can redirect the path
Chosen for me and fallen
Ungracefully

I know I can make things right
To see through and mend the past
To be the first for the first time
To be the last never

Crystal Blue

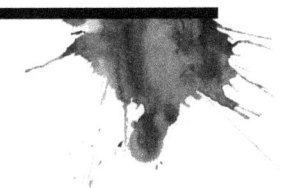

Slip down
Step aside
Take with you
Crystal blue
The perfect view

Separate
To bring together
Look at one another
Take it all apart
Where to start
Collide with people
Plastic hearts

Change it
Where to go
Emulate
To situate
Then look
And once again the other
Communicate

How to
When, what, why
Waste nothing
Look out
To look within
Take with you
A perfect view

Crystal blue

Talking

Hide true feelings
A mask made by others
Never growing
Never knowing
True thoughts, perceptions, intentions
Just keep talking with a smile
Subtly tell of embarrassing uncertainties
To find the missing pieces of the mind
To find the strength with words
To find the light in the darkness

The Pulse

The pulse, sleeping, beating
For the dream, yearning, waiting
There are no signs from the hand on the pulse

Growing older
Eyes see dimly
Becoming colder
That time back when
The eyes see dimly
And so does the mind

In the dream, seeing, believing
In the pulse, tainted, fading
In the mind, an image, eclectic
From the pulse in a dream

I want to fade into the dream
Feel the pulse consume me
Beating heart, rushing, pulsing
Imagine, I can do anything
Consume the dream
Consuming me
Unleash the pulse
That breaks me
And makes me

The Urge to Break

Tilted on axis
Staggering on the fault line
I stumble
Tread in the flesh to pierce the bloodline
Picking fresh scabs again

I lie, hiding from the truths
These truths I already knew
Losing the will to pursue a life
I always wanted

Standing on the floodgates
Swimming through the rivers
These channels of the brain
Carrying all my stones and boulders
The weight of it all drags me down beneath the depths
Treading in the mind to pierce the memory
Picking fresh scabs again

Losing the will to carry on
But I must have the urge to break free
Break the cycle from those who have lost
Their will to pursue the lives they always wanted

Now battered and broken
They lie here, hiding from truths
They thought they knew
Losing their will to carry on
They held me back, but I must have the urge

Scabs can heal if left alone, I'll see
Wings will dry
I'll learn to fly, little bird

Have the urge to break free!

About the Author

Keith Levesque is a creative writer, musician, and teacher from Westport, Massachusetts. Keith spent most of his early childhood moving around to different homes and schools and had a lot of time alone with his thoughts and observations. Not content to hold his thoughts in his head, Keith found creative outlets to pour out these musings.

Most recently, Keith has taught and lived in Korea and Japan. His former band, Asleep Without Dreaming (AWD) broke into the South Korean indie rock scene where AWD experienced recognition as an upcoming indie band. AWD released a full-length original album called Forever Endeavor and appeared on NHK TV, Busan City radio, and Groove Korea magazine. Keith later formed Adamtree and released an original song, Two Ships. His current project is a creative podcast called Mystics at Midnight, and he has an infinite amount of other creative projects planned for the future.

Additional Resources

Additional Resources

You may follow me or my current and previous projects through the links below;

Keith Levesque
https://www.facebook.com/keith.levesque.12/
keithlevesque83 (Instagram)

Adamtree
https://www.facebook.com/adamtreeband/
adamtreeband (Instagram)

Adamtree – Two Ships
https://youtu.be/493sgjrn83M

Podcast

Asleep Without Dreaming – You Move Me (Official Music Video)
https://youtu.be/Q8nfNOPPmi4

Asleep Without Dreaming – Wither Without
https://youtu.be/cw1YuxPwdhs

www.ingramcontent.com/pod-product-compliance
Lightning Source LLC
Chambersburg PA
CBHW061331040426
42444CB00011B/2872